About the Author

Mbeke Wasame (formerly Sharon Bell) is a mother, writer, trainer, educational consultant, and coach. She wrote poetry as a student in secondary school and was awarded second place in the 1979 Black Penmanship competition for her poem 'What being black means to me'.

In 1981, Mbeke (then Sharon) wrote 50% of the songs that were part of the theatre production Motherland. Elyse Dodgeson who developed powerful oral history techniques using improvisation, testimony and context, directed this. She asked her pupils to interview women who had come to Britain from the Caribbean in the 1950s – mostly their mothers and this research became Motherland, a landmark piece of verbatim theatre, performed by the girls from Vauxhall Manor, at the Oval House Theatre in Kennington in 1982.

Mbeke's first book of poetry was published in 1987, *Exploring all of me*, which was then followed by *Make the changes and feel the joy*, a personal development book, in 2014. She was a regular contributor to 72M magazine during 2011-2016. *How to work and live abroad successfully* was released as an e-book in 2019.

Mbeke is a Writer, international Educational Consultant, Coach, and Trainer. She has lived and worked in Cameroon, Ghana, Jamaica, Malaysia and in the UK.

Her most recent work appears in the anthology *Home* 2019, *This is Us, Black British and Female* 2019 and *Trusted Black Girl, Challenging Perceptions and Maximising the Potential of Black Women in the UK Workplace* by Roianne Nedd (2018).

She has a body of articles that have appeared in Black Business and Culture magazine, Pambazuka, the Alarm magazine and 72M magazines. She now contributes to Diversity Business and Turning Point magazine.

Mbeke is an established short stories writer who has had work published by *Fifth Estate, Pure Slush, Dovetails,* and *The Writers Café.*

With her writing and traveling experience, she is now working on an anthology of writing by women who have lived and worked abroad.

EXPLORING ALL OF ME

85 POEMS ON RACE, GENDER, CLASS AND CULTURE

MBEKE WASEME
FKA SHARON BELL

GLOBAL CHANGE CONSULTANTS

Exploring All of Me copyright © Sharon Bell aka Mbeke Waseme
Second edition published 2019 by Global Change Consultants

All rights reserved by the author and publisher. Except for brief excerpts used for review or scholarly purposes, no part of this book may be reproduced in any manner whatsoever without express written consent of the publisher or the author.
Any historical inaccuracies are made in error.

ISBN: 978-1-925536-83-6

Global Change Consultants
77 St Williams Way
Rochester ME1 2NY
UNITED KINGDOM

Email: Globalchangeconsultants@gmail.com
Website: http://www.mbekewaseme.com/

GLOBAL CHANGE CONSULTANTS
Global Us. International You

Photographs by Amenah Waseme, Richard Chin and Mbeke Waseme
Picture (back cover) of the author holding the original publication of *Exploring All of Me* was taken by Rohan Lawrence at The Black Cultural Archives, Brixton, London. The BCA was established by Len Garrison who created the Black penmanship competition.

Cover design recreated by Matt Potter

Also available as an eBook
ISBN: 978-1-925536-84-3

This book is dedicated
to my children, to my family
and to the world that continues
to provide me with
daily amazing content.

About this Book

Exploring all of me was originally published in 1987. Mbeke (then known as Sharon) was 22 years old. She had completed her degree at The University of Sussex at 21 and returned to live in South East London. She was single and looking for a place to spend her weekends after another week in a job that offered her little opportunity for creativity or growth.

Peckham Bookplace was a busy community space where international speakers performed, political discussions took place, Adult Education learning happened and something exciting was always going on. It was in the centre of an area whose demographic was predominantly African and Caribbean people with the highest number of young people from West Africa in London. This part of London is called Southwark.

The young women's writing group on a Saturday attracted her as she was young and liked to write! The Bookplace was also local to where she lived so she could walk there. This was important as a walker, she was able to have her walking meditation space where she could immerse herself in the environment, hear the birds singing, see the plants growing and observe the changes that were happening all around her. And of course, it provided her with content for her writing!

The facilitators of the group were amazing and she has great memories of Judy McClune and Richard Gray screaming with enthusiasm as she read out her new poems. This motivated her to write more and more and more. The group had funding to produce an anthology. However, between herself and one other member of the group, she wrote so much that it was decided that they should have their own books.

Now, in her glowing 50s, Mbeke feels very blessed to have had this opportunity. She knows exactly what her younger self was thinking! She is able to look at herself in her 20s and reconnect with the values, ideas, and insight. She is impressed! Her son has always said that she was born old and, he may be right.

Much of what she wrote in her 20s, still resonates with her. Some things have changed and the style through which she articulates her ideas has certainly changed. She puts this down to age, travel and new learning which has affected her in many ways. Some of the core ideas still hold true three decades on.

The original book was produced with the financial assistance of Greater London Arts, the London Borough of Southwark Women's Committee, John Collett's Educational Foundation, and the London Association for the Teaching of English.

This republished version is a self-publishing project.

Judy, Richard and I in the UK summer of 2019

Mummy, I am
growing — can you see me growing
into a woman
of blackness
and strange conquest.

Mummy, I am
growing — can you see me growing
into a woman
of blackness
and strange conquest.

Contents

My Introduction	1
Poetry and Me	3
It Doesn't Make It Right	4
If …	6
We Sat Talking	8
What the Fuck …?	9
Tomorrow	11
Civil Service Application Form	14
The Man	16
Joanne	18
Gone	19
Just Like a Man	20
You Can't Tell Me	21
Said Before – But True Same Way	23
Checkin You Out	25
Spiritually: Dedicated to Michael	27
The Ones I Miss	28
What About The Men Who Write	29
Yes	30
Life	31
You Knew (You Would Have Understood)	32
Time	34
To My Sisters	36
Black Tradition	38
I Need to Shit You Out	39
For You – Me?	40
Mummy	41
Writing	44
Strength Together, Strength Apart	46

It Was Never Said	47
One Year After	48
There Is Such a Difference ...	50
Remember Me?	52
My Choice	53
Maybe	55
I Won't Wait	56
You Know	57
I'm Still Hurting Mama	58
The Colours of Life	59
Poetshee	60
Neglect From Both	62
You Don't Understand	64
Daddy Why?	65
My Pen and I	66
Greatest Love of All	67
Christmas	69
Exploring All of Me	70
Walk Away	71
Sussex 1985	72
Truth and Strength	76
So So Illogical	77
I Think!	78
To Those Who Helped ...	80
Justice For You	83
Black Mistory!	85

My Introduction

I am not established
yet,
and
I
am not known.
My name is
not
Walker or
Morrison
or Shange or
Davies
It is Sharon.
Look
at it good,
Spell it the way
my Mother has
and,
if you have time,
recognise me for
what l am,
What am I?
I am an expression of my life.

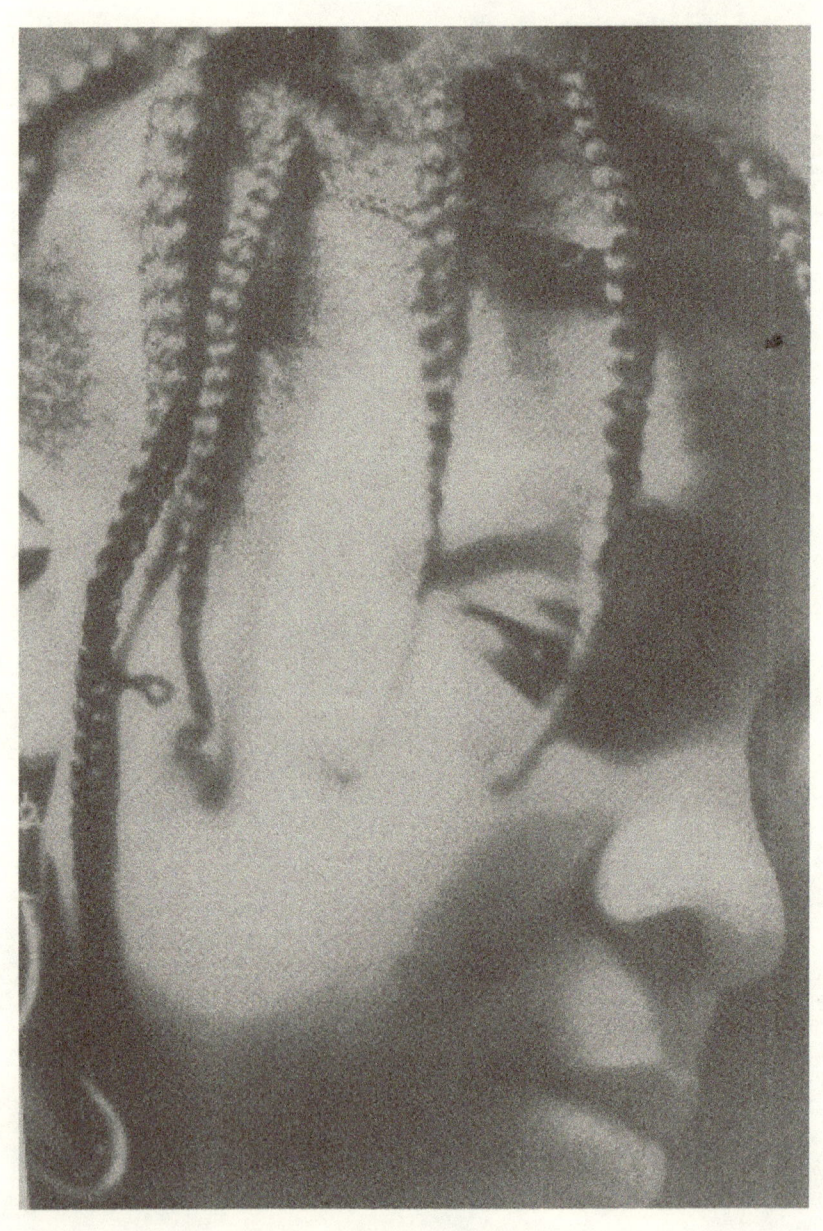

Sharon Bell (aged 22)

Poetry and Me

People always
sayin'
I can't write
like you —
I ain't no poet.

I laugh!
I never meant to
be no poet either.

It just crept in
and had the
effect of a
long hot bath
or a long
stroll in the park
and it felt
SO good.

I HAD to keep
going back
for more of that
good stuff

Poetry just got a
hold on me.

It Doesn't Make It Right

For years black people been
straightening their hair
Those years don't make it right
For years white people wrote
their version of history
They say Jesus Christ was white
For years Africa was the
black unknown
And this only damaged our sight
For the last few years we've
seen they were wrong
So now we're reclaiming our right.

For years white people
have been at the top
Those years don't make it right
For years women have been
begging the men to stop
It's not them they're s'pose to fight
For years we've wanted and
couldn't afford to get
But those years don't make it right
For years we've watched the children
While each heart stood and fret
Not knowing what could happen come night

Those years keep coming and
Those years pass by
We laugh, we love, we live, we cry
What most of us don't check is
that things can change
Because it's been so — it don't must stay the same
For years it's been so but
those years don't make it right.

If ...

If I came to you
and cried,
or begged forgiveness
or lay down to die
thru' lack of happiness,
Would you — now think
Would you respect me?
I think not.
Your male 'isms' would require
the dignity of 'woman'
to hold strong and just ga long.

If you came to me;
if you cried, or
hesitated because
life was a lie,
I'd lay down beside you
and offer
you my happiness,
I'd lay down so you could
hide between my legs.
To be away from the rest of the world
and,
I'd try to show you,
I love you ...

I'd allow the boy in your soul
to drain the remains of my mother
an
I'd still ga long ...
I'd still be strong.

We Sat Talking

We sat talking
all night
about our
beautiful female
friends.

You wanted to
test my jealousy,
My 'devotion' to
you
Speaking of long
legs, while mine
are short
and of nice
figures, while
I hated mine.

Did you ever think
that the other
woman could be
my lover as well
as yours —
Obviously not!

What the Fuck …?

We lay down
and we
prepare to
make love.
We prepare
to give
and receive
and sooth
and believe
that this
act, if pleasurable,
will bring
a
better tomorrow.

I ask you.,
how many times
has this proved
no more than
mere illusion.
Instead — WE FUCK!

We bang!
We bump!
We Grind!

We unwind!
All of which
are understandably(!)
explained
by the fact
that we
are residents of
a fucked-up
screwed up
society!!
This results
In our
expressive
cry for love
turning Into
mere fucking!!!

If we can learn
To spend time
simply touching
and experiencing
'feelings',
We can learn to love.
We can learn to make love.

Tomorrow

Times are CHANGING if
we see what
lies a head.
Times are SURELY changing
just tek time —
You'll see the change.

We been dung on di
rock fi SO long,
Ain't no way tings stayin
di same.
Talking blues won't be di
children dem song,
just tek time —
You'll see the change.

Tomorrow is SEE REE US —
if you really know what I mean,
Decisions will HAVE
to be made.
Time for DEAF IN ISH ONS
of weh we striving to
Too LONG we still playing
dis game.

Black people have gone
full circle.
REE A LISING what a
hypocrite white philosophy has been,
With such an incredible denial of
CULTURE
Black people will never know just
WHAT COULD HAVE BEEN.

In providing us wid false views,
we're not sure whether we've
lost or gained merit,
Messing up our heads wid
more false trut bout
how EX TEN SHION BEGIN WID
BO DERICK!

Laugh you laugh me idren,
Is noh joke!
A serious manipulation a gwan;
Now we a try fe reclaim fe we
culture,
white man waan fe laugh we to
SCORN.

Any strent mus come from di
FUTURE — di future based
on di PASS.
Tomorrow will build to a stronger
NEXT year;
Is jus a pity we might haffi see
blood shed TO DE LAS ...

Civil Service Application Form

Civil service
application form
waan fe know weh
I woman born.

Civil service
application form
waan fe know is
weh my madda
come from.

Civil service
application form
waan feh know if
I is british by birt.

Civil service
application form
waan fe know if I shall
inherit di eart!

Civil service
application form
have much front,
I woman seh,
Dem ask, if madda
deceased, a weh
she did stay!

Listen Mr Civil service,
I don't know is
wah you game —
You waan too much
infemashion, beside
mi name.
It sad fe tink seh
competishion get
so tough dat
application information
start fe require all
dat stuff!
Civil service
application form,
I mek a decishion —
I a sen you right
back to weh you
did come from!!

The Man

The man
don't belong to
NO ONE and
as the two
women in his life
it's something we
got to understand.
He don't have
two to belong
to one
He done got two
so he can do
what HE
wants to do —
either to me or he
can do it to you.

Joanne

The women blame the
women so the men
don't get no blame
So many things changing
while so many stay
the same.

Gone

I had a love for you
I was scared so
I held it in my hand
I was scared
Can you understand?

I had a love for you
it was small
till it grew and grew
but I was scared
So I didn't give it to you.

I have a love for you
But my fear sent you away
Maybe I'll save it for another Sunday
Maybe it will slowly dissolve away
Maybe in my hand it will stay.

Just Like a Man

As I lay beside you
Rejecting your rejection
You shattered me to
tears - you turned
my independent world
into a worthless conquest
of maleness.

Just like a man
  — in wanting to be independent
  — in wanting to be loved on my terms
  — in having had more than one lover
  (while you had lost count)
I was just like a man!!

Mister
you didn't realise that I
am ME — trying to find who I
am and trying to find strength
in BEING who I am
As a Woman — Is this SO Wrong???

You Can't Tell Me

You question me
        about my music
and you quizz me
        on reggae music past
You tell me how
        you've lived in Africa
And patronise about
how non-violence
        Would never last.

You quote my people's
        words
from a purely intellectual
  stance
You analyse and compartmentalise
our ancestral African
        dance.

You tell me you know
        better
Your knowledge of me
is greater than mine
Well, I say
        You should tek a back seat
My history is not for 'discussion'
as you dine!

My feelings come from within
The drum still calls to me
It's not from an analytical
        stance
It is the bondage of
the enslaved and unfree.

No chains historians say
And yes, it cannot be denied
        but civilisation's
chains are greater
Though free life is entwined.

You people — all of you
call yourselves as you may
Remember, no library can teach you experience,
Experience we gain day by day.

Said Before – But True Same Way

You clean de white man
office, and you clean
de white man flat,
a whole heap a politics
lay dung behin a dat.

You watch de white man
tele and you follow
de white man trend;
a whole heap a black
people a go see
a wicked end.

You use de white man
language an don't
realise seh you a
niggerize you self
'De politics of language
need a place upon you shelf.

You check de white man
beauty — bout you a
straighten up you head,
You no check seh black
a beauty — mek white man
whitewash you instead.

You an you an you is
all a you me a chat to
You an you an you I seh I know you na hear noting new
but one day someting a go
lick you, an one day you a go
see seh it true.

Checkin You Out

I was just
        checkin you out,
Wasn't that
        what you said?
Just checkin you out,
Had no intention
        on no bed;
Just checkin you out
to see what's in your head.

You made me laugh
        brother black,
I tell you true.
Asking if I could see
We're under attack,
        I was also checkin you
I could see what you
was after
I saw what you wanted
to do.

You was strong on the
      revolution,
Back to Africa like
Garvey say,
You mentioned black
      man in evolution
And foresaw a black
      Africa one day.
You asked if I'd share
      some sensi
then asked if I
      wanted to stay!

Now a message to
      all black brothers,
You see, everybody's
      checkin everbody out
So, when we get together,
      there ain't no need to spout.
I'm beginning to come to terms
      With what some of you's all about
So, next time you check a sister
      No see if de sister also a check you out!

Spiritually:
Dedicated to Michael

Spiritually
You see into
me Spiritually
you show me
how life could
be Spiritually
you tell me
of the me
I will be in
time Spiritually
I open to your
voice and let
you teach me
life Spiritually.

The Ones I Miss

I'm so mad
cause
I forgot to
write
it down,
Now it's
floating with
the stars
And
I'll never
Get it
To Ground.

What About The Men Who Write

I know you're out there
Even though you're far and few
I know you feel the pain
And release the anguish as I do.

To all the men who write
My respect goes out to you.

Yes

The games we play have
no gender
the jealously we feel —
only we can remember,
More babies will be born
come next September.

Life

If I learn to
live for today
and never worry
about the past
I will feel less
pain and,
strength will come
to me because
I choose to live
                for
                the
                future.

You Knew (You Would Have Understood)

You would have understood
because you knew me like
I do — you would
have understood because
you are you
You would know how

to see me through
because you knew I had
love for you
You would have understood
it's true.

Time

Time.
In weeks gone by
you have, strayed
far.
I miss you Time.

Do you remember,
long wintry nights
where we
had each
other?
I miss you time.
Do you remember
early
morning-
Yes, even before
the sun came
to greet us?
I miss you time.

But I wait.
I know
you are my
friend and,
like old friends,
we shall one day
meet again.

To My Sisters

I have tried to give
the children courage and
I have tried to show
them the way.
The children — they must
know that black is strong
To look to a picture
and say "mummy she is like
me" is strength.
We show weakness and
encourage shame if
all surrounding images
show a whiteness you
can only aspire to be.
Black we are and
we must teach the children.
Our strength will come
from our acceptance of ourselves.
Sisters, the children have
a world to build — give them the tools
for their foundation.

Black Tradition

I wash my
clothes and I
cook my
food — I keep
doin all these
things cause black
tradition feel so
good! I soak
my peas and I
strip my fish, just
keep seasoning my
meat cause tradition
feel so good. I tie
my head and stay
natural instead — black
woman got nuff pride
and I don't
intend to step aside
so I just keep strong
and as I is going on
Black tradition gi me pride.

I Need to Shit You Out

I need to
SHIT you out
of my SYSTEM!
You're CONSTIPATING
my thoughts,
I need to get
rid of this bunged-up feeling
And really clean
out my ARSE!

For You – Me?

When you rape me
tonight
and walk away
Satisfied,
will you think of
Me
Tonight?

Pleasure for two,
they never taught
it to you.

Mummy

Mummy, you were black
Only, I never thought of you as proud
For, if proudness is so visible
I don't remember seeing yours.
You were fat,
like all the others.
It seemed like all
West-Indian mothers were fat.
The white mothers were the figure conscious
and, it was a sort of
unspoken fact.
You were so secretive
As if all your thoughts
lay under your wig and scarf.
You said you were happy,
You never said you were sad.
You regretted having so many children
And, then
I question If you did.
I mean mummy,
How was your life?
Did it hurt to be left to cope?
You never said.
You said I was rude
We were the worst kids in the world.

That hurt, and I ask
just how true was that statement to you.
You seemed not to know how to laugh
Not to show the other side of your emotion.
I was tired of your anger
Your hurt.
I was hurt too.
Did you realise that I
was hurt too?

I wonder if I loved you.
I wonder if, yes.
just how much of my love I was giving to you.
Did you love me?
Did you realise the damage you did.
My colour,
Did you know how I
hated my colour for a while in my life.
How I hated the split between me and another,
just because of my colour.
You cussed me and. yes,
I know all mothers do.
You said that my stomach would be
 soon full of babies.
For really, my life would be like one big whore.
You never stopped,
You just kept pressuring me more.

Did you love me?
I wish I could know
because we both hurt each other.
and who the hell I can blame
I still don't know.
And now
trying to make a success of my life,
You're not here to show.
I hope though, that
If your life had been spared
You could love just as I want to.
Maybe, if you were here today
I'd probably be elsewhere.
Yet, the poem has no end
for the end hasn't reached
At least, not for me ...

Writing

PENCIL
TO PAPER
TO BEGIN
FOR BIRTH
TO RECREATE
AFTER DEATH
FOREVER.

PEN
TO PAPER
TO CONIFIRM
TO SHOW
I HAVE LEARNED
AND AM STILL WALKING
THE PATH TO LEARN

Strength Together, Strength Apart

Let us kneel
and
face
the world
so we can
face each
other
in the world
so we can
learn to be
alone
and be
together
in the world.

It Was Never Said

We never really said
goodbye so we
haven't really been
apart. Goodbye
would seal and
protect emotions.
Now instead we
break the heart.

One Year After

One year ago — we were one
Now we are two
fear of losing even the
friendship we once had
fear of awkward meetings
and desperate pleas
can you
hear   me
calling   you
can I hear
you
calling   me
somewhere ...
nowhere ...
maybe ...
we'll
see
The hands of time
only go forward
it's a shame
I'd played the
game and
made the
rules.

I now know
what it is
to experience
love — I
know you
loved me; maybe
even
still
love
me.

There Is Such a Difference …

I have
shared my
body with …
I have
made love
with few ….

Remember Me?

Remember me
I am the one you will
never forget
Remember me
I am the woman who
was more independent
than you, more outgoing
than you and more
outspoken than you.
Remember me
I am the one who
loved then left
(the one who you said would
always love and leave)
Remember me
I am forever remembering you.

My Choice

Do I need
to bear
a child in order
to be a whole
Must I
Experience
growth
of womb
to satisfy
your soul

Your soul ... Your soul ...

Must I follow
natural path,
dispose of all
contraceptive pills
suddenly start to
love you —
forgetting all your
ills
Must I bear weight
nine months
or be seven for
premature birth —

Do I alone bear
this cross as a
result of sexual
violent pain

Think again… Think again …

OK, not always violent
but the joy of pain
— know what I mean —
when you hurt me like you do
Do you hear how loud I scream
Child birth — I'll leave it for a while
Got to get to grips with me first

Satisfy my thirst … Satisfy my thirst

Maybe

Maybe, through all the
use and abuse
I can no longer
see a friend and
Maybe, if friendship was
tripping me over I
would still choose to
bypass it thru'
fear of hurt
Maybe ...
Oh, it all seems so
foggy and so clear.

I Won't Wait

I won't wait for
you because you
will never know
what it is
to
wait
for
me
I won't cry for you
as you will never know
what if feels like to
cry
for
me
I won't do for you what
you won't do for me because
longing for you drains
away my energy

You Know

Still so much
unsaid and we
just go on and
on and hope ...
One day we will
release the ghost
from the past
and we will be
well and truly
free ...
Until that time
Comes we can
only make do with
what we allow ...
We are the ones who
hold our selves back.

I'm Still Hurting Mama

I'm still hurting mama
still hurting
still weeping
still crying
still waiting
for you mama.

I'm still hoping
you'll say
if 's alright
I'm still hoping
still praying
that somewhere
you're loving me

still hoping mama
still
waiting

The Colours of Life

ANGER
 COMPELS
ME TO DEEP
PURPLE YOU!

JOY ALLOWS
ME TO
BRIGHT ORANGE YOU.

BLACK HOLDS ME
 STRONG.
IT ALLOWS ME TO
 TURN FROM
YOU
TURN TO
 YOU
AND NEVER
                      LOOK BACK.

Poetshee

I looked
at mine;
turned,
examined it,
and
looked good.
'POETSHEE'!
That's what
I'd call
it;
POETSHEE!

Having had
this thing
follow we
for most of
my life
and it
now
representing
such a
mirror
of my life,

It should
rightfully
have a name.

I call it
POETSHEE

Neglect From Both

We are one
yet
we are divided.

I, as a
black, woman
must reject
you both.

Feminism with
an 18th century English
history
has nothing to
help me live.

The civil
rights and revolution
forgot to
mention the women
what the heck
happened to all
those black women
during that time?

Both causes —
both fights —
forgot to make room
for the black women.

It seems, during
all of this, I
was just too god damn
busy being strong!!

You Don't Understand

You don't
understand I
keep
sayin to
you
you don't
understand.

You think I
hated
you
I never
hated
you.
I loved
you.

It was just
that
hate
was
an
easier
emotion
to
express.

Daddy Why?

Daddy don't touch
me when you know it
ain't right
Daddy don't do
that cause I'm
afraid of you tonight
Why do mummy got
to work
Always leaving us
alone
I is only a baby
and this will surely
mash up the home.

Oh daddy I is afraid
Not only what you do to
mother
Daddy I is afraid
cause you represent the father
the Uncle, the Brother.

My Pen and I

Let's write
pen
Let's be friends
again
and
let's
get
as close
as
we can
possibly be.

If you want to
cry,
sigh,
shout,
scream,
we can
work together.

We can,
(delete),
We are
together.

Greatest Love of All

The greatest
love of all —
to love me!
to love you is
not so great
after all!

Christmas

Since,
I have no love
for white Christ,
I shall not celebrate
your Christ-mas
but,
I have love
for those who love me
and
since,
on looking back
December 25th
now represents a
day where
we try — we make
the effort to be together
and,
we love,
I shall celebrate
in my own way
and be happy
because we can share.

Exploring All of Me

De 'I' is black
an de I n I
feels rastafari.
De I is Jamaican,
African, English —
a mixture of blood
and culture and
knowledge. De
me is so many
tings — individually and
consciencely a part.
De me is striving
inna forward
direction so dat
de 'I' can be
strong.

Walk Away

I thought ...
it doesn't
matter
now,
I suppose, I
suppose I thought ...
I remember
waiting.
Long hours of
no sleep
and times
of complete
oblivion
to the
rest of
the world.
Anxious
and
stagnant.
Waiting,
I thought ...
I stopped thinking!
I knew!
I was *ANGRY*
and
you
were definitely
to blame.

Sussex 1985

Your sentence
is three
years.
Unlike
closed walls,
there
is
open
space.
Unlike
good behaviour,
early
release
depends
on
bad
behaviour.
Unlike
single sexed,
there
is
every sex.

If we call
it a
three year
'experiment',
there are
bound to
be 'results'.

The results
are that we
grow.
Taking into
account that
growth works
two ways —
we grow.

The top of
the tree
no longer seems
so high, so we
fly to nest.
Taboos of expression
are unleased
so we express.
The invisible boundaries
appear to say
this is your
quest.

Others hide —
Cover their eyes
and hide.
Many need a
quo where the
game is clearly
mapped.
No walls can
equal no foundation
can equal no
stability — they
crumble and fall
away at the side.
They close themselves
away — they hide.
Three years turns
to four — or more
or more.

Your sentence is
three years.
Unlike closed walls,
there is open
space.

Truth and Strength

The inner love
of truth — it
is the right of
each and own
your truth belongs
to no one else
cause only you tell
the truth alone

Your strength comes
from belief and
you believe in your
own truth — it don't
matter if you're
woman, man, or child
or youth.

They belong as does
your name — becoming
part of you just
the same. We must
learn our inner depth
in order to learn our
potential truth and to know
our inner strength.

So So Illogical

I am so
illogical I cannot
stand myself!
I allowed the half inch,
spider to move nine
stones of me to sleep
next door.
It was surprising how
little it had to say —
being there was plenty.

I Think!

I'm going to
make my move
so I
think.
I'm ready to
make my approach
so I
think.
I sit back
and realize
that 'equality'
alone
cannot
untie the
chains that
bound me.
Women's 'liberation'
cannot
cushion
the pain
when you say
'no'
female 'emancipation'
cannot
cover my shame
if you whisper
and laugh to your
friends.

I ask
when will
it end

The power ...
The power ...

Male world,
if you call
me slut,
I feel like
nothing;

I question my
actions, my approach,
my attire,
your satire
This world ...

If
It can be so
I can approach
you,
society must
see me as it
can see you.
My actions must
be taken
for granted;
in fact,
they must be
'Matter-of-fact'.

To Those Who Helped ...

to those of you
who helped
I hope

you are
now
proud.

To those of
you who
stood back,

pat
yourself
on
the
back.

You have
created
history

or
herstory

depending
on
the
political
side
you feel
you be.

DESTRUCTION
OF A NATION

an achievement
in itself.

DESTRUCTION
OF A
NATION

you must be so
proud of
'one's-self'

DESTRUCTION
OF A
NATION

with a gold
medal to
place on one's
self.

Justice For You

They don't judge you like
they judge me
Preconceptions layed to grow
They will make false accusations
But, on knowing this
They'll let it go

They don't judge you like
they judge me
Colour ain't got no where to hide
Dungarees and short cropped hair cuts
Won't give me an easier ride.

They don't judge you like
they judge me
Made sure old slavery saw
to that
And in maintaining white south
Africa
They show how Black women will stay
in receipt of attack.

They don't judge you like
they judge me
because to arse that
wouldn't do
If dem a show respect
to tatcher
Dem can't really check fe Ms
Truth* too.

In fact, let's lay it down
This judgement ain't fair at all
While my history bury underground
Your history stand great and tall
So judgement will never be equal
While the evidence is weighed for you
and in a way I well understand why a
fair-equal-judgement just would not do.

* Sojourner Truth

Black Mistory!

If 'dark' was 'pure'
and virginal black
was the in thing,
this country would be
whitist England making
darkist Africa the place to be!

Black could be unstained,
innocent, harmless, GOOD,
POSITIVE, instead of
dirty, deadly. SINISTER,
WICKED.

We have to realise that
the white man went to
a lot of trouble to make
black a conceptual term
weighted heavily with shame.

We — yes you and I
have a task to reverse
the damage before we
go forward stronger.
It is up to those who see
to teach those who
cannot.

A Note from the Author

Exploring all of me was originally published in 1987. In 1989, I was invited to the US by the Adult Literacy group, to deliver a number of poetry readings and workshops in Boston, New York and Washington.

On completing these sessions, I would often board the plane in my usual excited and enthusiastic way. I was so empowered by this journey, the opportunity to share my poetry and the positive feedback I had received.

This day was no different as I relaxed into my seat, took out my diary and was about to begin journaling. The elderly black gentleman at the end of my row looked at me and asked if he could have my diary. I paused at his request and, although I thought it was strange, I still said yes! He wrote this on the back page of my book. We never spoke. He simply wrote this, handed the diary back to me and went back to reading his book.

It inspires me to this day.

I continue to be grateful for the opportunities, confidence, and confirmation which having *Exploring all of me* published at 22, bought to my life.

6/6/89 4/6/89

From the first time I saw you there was a light in your life that I could not identify. Your beauty overwhelms me. It touches my entire being. I will never, ever see you again but the mere presence of your being has given me hope for tomorrow. A poet is unique, with a message that is old as life, yet new and fresh as the new day.

Your fresh words, thoughts, smile makes me know that life continues in a special way that I have never known before. What is the source of your light? I will never know. But to harness it, hold it for a short time would be eternal.

You are unique and special. Continue those God gifted talents, and many people's lives will be changed, mobilized to act, and challenged to see the world differently.

E. McNair

Transcript

4/6/89

From the first time I saw you there was a light in your life that I could not identify. Your beauty overwhelms me. It touches my entire being. I will never see you again but the mere presence of your being has given me hope for tomorrow. A poet is unique, with a message that is as old as life, yet new as the new day.

Your fresh words, thoughts, smile makes me know that life continues in a special way that I have never known before. What is the source of your light? I will never know. But to harness it, hold it for a short time would be eternal.

You are unique and special. Continue those God-given talents and many people's lives will be changed, mobilized to act and challenged to see the world differently.

G. McNair

Judy McClune was part of the first book and was there with me adding the final touches to this republished version.

www.ingramcontent.com/pod-product-compliance
Lightning Source LLC
Chambersburg PA
CBHW031410040426
42444CB00005B/501